The Official Rules of Soccer

TRIUMPH
BOOKS
CHICAGO

These Official Laws of the Game have been approved by the
International Football Association Board. (The I.F.A.B. is the
international ruling body for Official Laws of the Game only.)

Cover photo: J. Brett Whitesell, RB Sports Photography
Typography: The Publishing Services Group

This book is available in quantity at special discounts for your
group or organization. For further information contact:

Triumph Books
644 South Clark Street
Chicago, Illinois 60605
312-939-3330
FAX 312-663-3557

Printed in Canada

U.S. Soccer Federation

The United States Soccer Federation, or U.S. Soccer, is the national governing body of soccer in the United States. With headquarters in Chicago, U.S. Soccer served as host federation for World Cup USA 1994, the most successful event in FIFA history.

U.S. Soccer was one of the world's first organizations to be affiliated with the Fédération Internationale de Football Association (FIFA), beginning in 1913. U.S. Soccer has continued to grow and now has the second-largest membership among U.S. Olympic Committee national governing bodies.

The first international soccer games to take place outside the British Isles were between the U.S. and Canada in 1885 and 1886, respectively, almost three decades prior to U.S. Soccer's formation. Soccer in the United States has come a long way since then.

Approximately fifty full-time U.S. Soccer employees work to administer and serve a membership located in all fifty states. Known originally as the U.S. Football Association, U.S. Soccer's name was changed to the United States Soccer Football Association in 1945 and then to its present name in 1974. U.S. Soccer is a non-profit, largely volunteer organization with much of its business administered by a national council of elected officials representing three administrative arms—approximately two million youth players

19 years of age and under; 300,000 senior players over the age of 19; and the professional division.

U.S. Soccer manages seven full national teams. Men's programs include the National Team, Under-23 (Olympic), Under-20, Under-17, and Five-A-Side. Women's teams include the National and Under-20 teams. Three developmental national team programs include Under-18 and Under-16 Boys and Under-18 Girls.

The host national association for the 1996 Olympic soccer matches, U.S. Soccer is proud of its many recent successes. The U.S. Women's National Team continued to make history by winning the first-ever gold medal in women's Olympic soccer. In 1991, the Women's National Team won the first-ever FIFA Women's World Championship in China. The Women's National Team captured the 1994 CONCACAF title to qualify for the 1995 world championship tournament in Sweden, where the team placed third, falling to eventual champion Norway 1-0 in the semifinal. The U.S. squad won U.S. Women's Cup '95, exacting a measure of revenge with an overtime victory over Norway in the final match.

The Men's National Team won the U.S. Cup '95 title and advanced to the semifinals of Copa America before bowing out to world-champion Brazil 1–0. The Men's National Team advanced to the second round of World Cup play in 1994 for the first time in 64 years.

Other recent U.S. Soccer achievements include the Indoor National Team capturing the silver medal at the FIFA Indoor Five-A-Side World Championship in November 1992 in Hong Kong; the Men's National Team winning the 1991

CONCACAF Gold Cup, winning the inaugural U.S. Cup '92 and defeating England 2-0 in U.S. Cup '93; the U-20 team finishing eighth in the 1993 FIFA Youth World Championship in Australia; and the Women's National Team finishing second in the 1993 World University Games in Buffalo, New York.

In 1997, two of U.S. Soccer's youth squads will contend for world titles. The U.S. Under-20 National Team will play at the World Youth Championship for the FIFA/Coca Cola Cup in Malaysia, while the U.S. Under-17s will travel to Egypt to compete for the Under-17 World Championship for the FIFA/JVC Cup.

Coaching schools are held regularly throughout the U.S. where interested persons may gain certification at six progressive levels. U.S. Soccer has more than 25,000 certified coaches. The Referee Program makes up an integral part of the United States soccer scene, with approximately 74,000 referees currently registered.

U.S. SOCCER FEDERATION
1801 South Prairie Avenue
Chicago, Illinois 60616 USA

Phone: 312/808-1300
Fax: 312/808-9566
E-mail: socfed@aol.com

Alan I. Rothenberg, *President*
Lawrence A. Monaco, Jr., *Executive Vice President*
Bill Goaziou, *Treasurer*
Hank Steinbrecher, *Secretary General/Executive Director*

Tom King, *General Manager*
Dan Flynn, *Chief Administrative Officer*

- National governing body for soccer in the United States.

- Non-profit organization founded in 1913.

- Largest membership in U.S. Olympic family.

- Approximately 3 million members.

- Fifty full-time staff at national headquarters in Chicago, thousands of volunteers nationwide to manage and implement programs at the youth and adult levels.

- Oversees 106 state offices (55 youth, 51 adult).

- Instrumental in making women's soccer an Olympic medal sport beginning in Atlanta 1996.

- Host federation for World Cup USA 1994 and the 1999 Women's World Championship.

- U.S. Women's National Team: 1991 FIFA World Champions; 1996 Olympic Champions.

- Operates 10 different national team programs:

Men	*Women*
National	*National/Olympic*
Olympic (U-23)	Under-20
Under-20	Under-16
Under-18	
Under-17	
Under-16	
Futsal	

Table of Contents

User's Guide

This edition of the Official Laws of the Game has been designed to give soccer fans of all ages a quick and easy reference guide to the action on the field.

Diagrams illustrating off-side points, instructions on taking kicks from the penalty-marks, and signals by the referee and linesmen can all be found here following the Laws themselves.

Please note that these rules are subject to the agreement of the National Associations as specified on the Notes page.

Notes

Subject to the agreement of the national association concerned and provided the principles of these Laws are maintained, the Laws may be modified in their application for matches for players of under 16 years of age, for women's football and for veterans' football (over 35 years).

Any or all of the following modifications are permissible:

(a) size of the field of play;

(b) size, weight and material of the ball;

(c) width between the goalposts and height of the cross-bar from the ground;

(d) the duration of the periods of play;

(e) number of substitutions.

Further modifications are only possible with the consent of the International Football Association Board.

References to the male gender in the Laws of the Game in respect of referees, assistant referees, players or officials are for simplification and refer to both males and females.

The Field of Play

The Field of Play

The field of play and appurtenances shall be as shown in the following plan:

(N. B. All measurements are in yards and inches unless otherwise marked.)

The Field of Play

(1) Dimensions. The field of play shall be rectangular, its length being not more than 130 yards nor less than 100 yards and its breadth not more than 100 yards nor less than 50 yards. (In international matches the length shall be not more than 120 yards nor less than 110 yards and the breadth not more than 80 yards nor less than 70 yards.) The length shall in all cases exceed the breadth.

(2) Marking. The field of play shall be marked with distinctive lines, not more than 5 inches in width (not by a V-shaped rut) in accordance with the plan, the longer boundary lines being called the touch-lines and the shorter the goal-lines. A flag on a post not less than 5 ft. high and having a non-pointed top, shall be placed at each corner; a similar flag-post may be placed opposite the half-way line on each side of the field of play, not less than 1 yard outside the touch-line. A halfway-line shall be marked out across the field of play. The centre of the field of play shall be indicated by a suitable mark and a circle with a 10 yards radius shall be marked round it.

(3) The Goal-Area. At each end of the field of play two lines shall be drawn at right-angles to the goal-line, 6 yards from each goal-post. These shall extend into the field of play for a distance of 6 yards and shall be joined by a line drawn parallel with the goal-line. Each of the spaces enclosed by these lines and the goal-line shall be called a goal-area.

(4) The Penalty-Area. At each end of the field of play two lines shall be drawn at right-angles to the goal-line, 18 yards from each goal-post. These shall extend into the field of play for a distance of 18 yards and shall be joined by a line drawn parallel with the goal-line. Each of the spaces enclosed by these lines and the goal-line shall be called a penalty-area. A suitable mark shall be made within each penalty-area, 12 yards from the mid-point of the goal-line, measured along an undrawn line at right-angles thereto. These shall be the penalty-kick marks. From each penalty-kick mark an arc of a circle, having a radius of 10 yards, shall be drawn outside the penalty-area.

(5) The Corner-Area. From each corner-flag post a quarter circle, having a radius of 1 yard, shall be drawn inside the field of play.

(6) The Goals. The goals shall be placed on the centre of each goal-line and shall consist of two upright posts, equidistant from the corner-flags and 8 yards apart (inside measurement), joined by a horizontal cross-bar the lower edge of which shall be 8 ft. from the ground.

For safety reasons, the goals, including those which are portable, must be anchored securely to the ground.

The width and depth of the cross-bars shall not exceed 5 inches (12 cm). The goal-posts and the cross-bars shall have the same width.

Nets [1] may be attached to the posts, cross-bars and ground behind the goals. They should be appropriately supported and be so placed as to allow the goal-keeper ample room.

---

[1] **Goal nets.** The use of nets made of hemp, jute or nylon is permitted. The nylon strings may, however, not be thinner than those made of hemp or jute.

Decisions of the International F.A. Board

(1) In international matches the dimensions of the field of play shall be: maximum 110 x 75 metres; minimum 100 x 64 metres.

(2) National associations must adhere strictly to these dimensions. Each national association organising an international match must advise the visiting association, before the match, of the place and the dimensions of the field of play.

(3) The Board has approved this table of measurements for the Laws of the Game:

130 yards	120 metres
120 yards	110
110 yards	100
100 yards	90
80 yards	75
70 yards	64
50 yards	45
18 yards	16.50
12 yards	11
10 yards	9.15
8 yards	7.32
6 yards	5.50
1 yard	1
8 feet	2.44
5 feet	1.50
28 inches	0.71
27 inches	0.68
9 inches	0.22
5 inches	0.12
3/4 inch	0.019
1/2 inch	0.0127
3/8 inch	0.010

14 ounces	396 grams
16 ounces	453 grams
8.5 lb./sq.in.	600 gr/cm^2
15.6 lb./sq.in.	1100 gr/cm^2

(4) The goal-line shall be marked the same width as the depth of the goal-posts and the cross-bar, so that the goal-line and goal-posts will conform to the same interior and exterior edges.

(5) The 6 yards (for the outline of the goal-area) and the 18 yards (for the outline of the penalty-area) which have to be measured along the goal-line, must start from the inner sides of the goal-posts.

(6) The space within the inside areas of the field of play includes the width of the lines marking these areas.

(7) All associations shall provide standard equipment, particularly in international matches, when the Laws of the Game must be complied with in every respect and especially with regard to the size of the ball and other equipment which must conform to the regulations. All cases of failure to provide standard equipment must be reported to FIFA.

(8) In a match played under the rules of a competition if the cross-bar becomes displaced or broken, play shall be stopped and the match abandoned unless the cross-bar has been repaired and replaced in position or a new one provided without such being a danger to the players. A rope is not considered to be a satisfactory substitute for a cross-bar.

In a friendly match, by mutual consent, play may be resumed without the cross-bar provided it has been removed and no longer constitutes a danger to the players. In these circumstances, a rope may be used as a substitute for a cross-bar. If a rope is not used and the ball crosses the goal-line at a point which, in the opinion of the referee is below where the cross-bar should have been, he shall award a goal.

The game shall be restarted by the referee dropping the ball at the place where it was when play was stopped, unless it was within the goal-area at that time, in which case it shall be dropped on that part of the goal-area line which runs parallel to the goal-line, at the point nearest to where the ball was when play was stopped.

(9) National associations may specify such maximum and minimum dimensions for the cross-bars and goal-posts, within the limits laid down in Law I, as they consider appropriate.

(10) Goal-posts and cross-bars must be made of wood, metal or other approved material as decided from time to time by the International F.A. Board. They may be square, rectangular, round, half-round or elliptical in shape.

Goal-posts and cross-bars made of other materials and in other shapes are not permitted. The goal-posts must be of white colour.

(11) Any kind of publicity is forbidden in connection with, or on, the field of play. In particular, no advertising material may be displayed at any level on nets, corner flags or goalposts, nor shall such appurtenances of the game have any extraneous equipment attached to them (cameras, microphones, etc.). The reproduction of a FIFA, Confederation, National Association, League,

Club or any other logo on the field of play (turf) is also forbidden.

(12) 'Curtain-raisers' to international matches should only be played following agreement on the day of the match, and taking into account the condition of the field of play, between representatives of the two associations and the referee (of the international match).

(13) National associations, particularly in international matches, should

- restrict the number of photographers around the field of play,
- have a line (photographers' line) marked behind the goal-lines at least two metres from the corner flag going through a point situated at least 3.5 metres behind the intersection of the goal-line with the line marking the goal-area to a point situated at least six metres behind the goal-posts,
- prohibit photographers from passing over these lines,
- forbid the use of artificial lighting in the form of "flashlights."

(14) A mark may be made off the field of play, 11 yards from the corner flag and at right angles to the goal-line, to help the referee ensure that this distance is observed when a corner kick is being taken.

The Ball

The Ball

The ball shall be spherical; the outer casing shall be of leather or other suitable materials. No material shall be used in its construction which might prove dangerous to the players. The circumference of the ball shall not be more than 70.0 cm and not less than 68.0 cm. The weight of the ball at the start of the game shall not be more than 450 g. nor less than 410 g. The pressure shall be equal to 0.6–1.1 atmosphere (=600–1,100g./cm²) at sea level. The ball shall not be changed during the game unless authorised by the referee.

Decisions of the International F.A. Board

(1) The ball used in any match shall be considered the property of the association or club on whose ground the match is played, and at the close of play it must be returned to the referee.

(2) The International Board, from time to time, shall decide what constitutes approved materials. Any approved material shall be certified as such by the International Board.

(3) The Board has approved these equivalents of the weights specified in the Law: 14 to 16 ounces = 396 to 453 grams.

(4) In FIFA competition matches and in competition matches under the auspices of the Confederations, acceptance of a football for use will be conditional upon the football bearing one of the following three designations:

- the official "FIFA APPROVED" logo, or
- the official "IFA INSPECTED" logo, or
- the reference "INTERNATIONAL MATCHBALL STANDARD"

Such designation on a football indicates that it was duly tested and found to be in compliance with the specific technical requirements for each category (FIFA APPROVED, FIFA INSPECTED and INTERNATIONAL MATCHBALL STANDARD, the latter being of equal technical standard to FIFA INSPECTED), additional to the minimum specifications set forth in Law II. The ball shall carry appropriate indication that it has been sucessfully tested. Such additional requirements, specific to each of the respective categories, have to be approved by the International F.A. Board. The institutes conducting the tests shall be selected by FIFA.

In all other matches the ball used must satisfy the requirements of Law II. National Associations or competitions may require the use of balls bearing any one of the three aforementioned designations.

(5) If the ball bursts or becomes deflated during the course of a match, the game shall be stopped and restarted by dropping the new ball at the place where the first ball became defective, unless it was within the goal-area at that time, in which case it shall be dropped on that part of the goal-area line which runs parallel to the goal-line, at the point nearest to where the ball was when play was stopped.

(6) If this happens during a stoppage of the game (place-kick, goal-kick, corner-kick, free-kick, penalty-kick or throw-in), the game shall be restarted accordingly.

Number of Players

SOCCER

Number of Players

(1) A match shall be played by two teams, each consisting of not more than eleven players, one of whom shall be the goalkeeper.

(2) Up to a maximum of three substitutes may be used in any match played in an official competition under the auspices of FIFA, the Confederations or the National Associations.

The rules of the competition shall state how many substitutes may be nominated, from three up to a maximum of seven.

The names of the substitutes must be given to the referee prior to the commencement of the match.

Substitutes not so named may not take part in the match.

(3) In other matches, up to five substitutes may also be used provided that the teams concerned reach an agreement on a maximum number, and that the referee is informed before the match. If the referee is not informed, or no agreement is reached before the commencement of the match, no more than three substitutes shall be permitted.

The names of the substitutes must be given to the referee prior to the commencement of the match.

(4) Any of the other players may change places with the goalkeeper, provided that the referee is informed before the change is made, and provided also that the change is made during a stoppage of the game.

(5) When a goalkeeper or any other player is to be replaced by a substitute, the following conditions shall be observed:

(a) The referee shall be informed of the proposed substitution, before it is made.

(b) The substitute shall not enter the field of play until the player he is replacing has left, and then only after having received a signal from the referee.

(c) He shall enter the field during a stoppage in the game, and at the halfway line.

(d) A player who has been replaced shall not take any further part in the game.

(e) A substitute shall be subject to the authority and jurisdiction of the referee whether called upon to play or not.

(f) The substitution is completed when the substitute enters the field of play, from which moment he becomes a player and the player whom he is replacing ceases to be a player.

Punishment:

(a) Play shall not be stopped for an infringement of paragraph 4. The players concerned shall be cautioned immediately the ball goes out of play.

(b) If a substitute enters the field of play without the authority of the referee, play shall be stopped. The substitute shall be cautioned and removed from the field or sent off according to the circumstances. The game shall be restarted by the referee dropping the ball at the place where it was when play was stopped, unless it was within the goal-area at that time, in which case it shall be dropped on that part of the goal-area line which runs parallel to the goal-line, at the point nearest to where the ball was when play was stopped.

(c) For any other infringement of this Law, the player concerned shall be cautioned, and if the game is stopped by the referee to administer the caution, it shall be restarted by an indirect free-kick, to be taken by a player of the opposing team from the place where the ball was when play was stopped, subject to the overriding conditions imposed in Law XIII.

| LAW III | **Decisions of the International F.A. Board** |

(1) The minimum number of players in a team is left to the discretion of national associatons.

(2) The Board is of the opinion that a match should not be considered valid if there are fewer than seven players in either of the teams.

(3) A player who has been ordered off before play begins may only be replaced by one of the named substitutes. The kick-off must not be delayed to allow the substitute to join his team.

A player who has been ordered off after play has started may not be replaced.

A named substitute who has been ordered off, either before or after play has started, may not be replaced.

(This decision only relates to players who are ordered off under Law XII. It does not apply to players who have infringed Law IV.)

Players' Equipment

Players' Equipment

(1) (a) The basic compulsory equipment of a player shall consist of a jersey or shirt, shorts, stockings, shinguards and footwear.

(b) A player shall not wear anything which is dangerous to another player.

(2) Shinguards, which must be covered entirely by the stockings, shall be made of a suitable material (rubber, plastic, polyurethane or similar substance) and shall afford a reasonable degree of protection.

(3) The goalkeeper shall wear colours which distinguish him from the other players and from the referee.

Punishment:

For any infringement of this Law, the player at fault shall be instructed to leave the field of play by the referee, to adjust his equipment or obtain any missing equipment, when the ball next ceases to be in play, unless by then the player has already corrected his equipment. Play shall not be stopped immediately for an infringement of this Law. A player who is instructed to leave the field to adjust his equipment or obtain missing equipment shall not return without first reporting to the referee, who shall satisfy himself that the player's equipment is in order. The player shall only re-enter the game at a moment when the ball has ceased to be in play.

| LAW IV | **Decisions of the International F.A. Board** |

(1) In international matches, international competitions, international club competitions and friendly matches between clubs of different national associations, the referee, prior to the start of the game, shall inspect the players' equipment and prevent any player whose equipment does not conform to the requirements of this Law from playing until such time as it does comply. The rules of any competition may include a similar provision.

(2) If the referee finds that a player is wearing articles not permitted by the Laws and which may constitute a danger to other players, he shall order him to take them off. If he fails to carry out the referee's instruction, the player shall not take part in the match.

(3) A player who has been prevented from taking part in the game or a player who has been sent off the field for infringing Law IV must report to the referee during a stoppage of the game and may not

enter or re-enter the field of play unless and until the referee has satisfied himself that the player is no longer infringing Law IV.

(4) A player who has been prevented from taking part in a game or who has been sent off because of an infringement of Law IV, and who enters or re-enters the field of play to join or re-join his team, in breach of the conditions of Law XII (j), shall be cautioned.

If the referee stops the game to administer the caution, the game shall be restarted by an indirect free-kick, taken by a player of the opposing side, from the place where the ball was when the referee stopped the game, subject to the overriding conditions imposed in Law XIII.

Referees

Referees

A referee shall be appointed to officiate in each game. His authority and the exercise of the powers granted to him by the Laws of the Game commence as soon as he enters the field of play.

His power of penalising shall extend to offences committed when play has been temporarily suspended, or when the ball is out of play. His decision on points of fact connected with the play shall be final, so far as the result of the game is concerned. He shall:

(a) enforce the Laws.

(b) refrain from penalising in cases where he is satisfied that, by doing so, he would be giving an advantage to the offending team.

(c) keep a record of the game; act as timekeeper and allow the full or agreed time, adding thereto all time lost through accident or other cause.

(d) have discretionary power to stop the game for any infringement of the Laws and to suspend or terminate the game whenever, by reason of the elements, interference by spectators, or other cause, he deems such stoppage necessary. In such a case he shall submit a detailed report to the competent authority, within the stipulated time, and in accordance with the provisions set up by the National Association under whose jurisdiction the match was played. Reports will be deemed to be made when received in the ordinary course of post.

(e) from the time he enters the field of play, caution and show a yellow card to any player guilty of misconduct or ungentlemanly behaviour. In such cases the referee shall send the name of the offender to the competent authority, within the stipulated time, and in accordance with the provisions set up by the national association under whose jurisdiction the match was played.

(f) allow no person other than the players and assistant referees to enter the field of play without his permission.

(g) stop the game if, in his opinion, a player has been seriously injured; have the player removed as soon as possible from the field of play, and immediately resume the game. If a player is slightly injured, the game shall not be stopped until the ball has ceased to be in play. A player who is able to go to the touch- or goal-line for attention of any kind, shall not be treated on the field of play.

(h) send off the field of play and show a red card to any player who, in his opinion, is guilty of violent conduct, serious foul play, the use of foul or abusive language, or is guilty of a second cautionable offence.

(i) signal for recommencement of the game after all stoppages.

(j) decide that the ball provided for a match meets with the requirements of Law II.

| LAW V | **Decisions of the International F.A. Board** |

(1) Referees in international matches shall wear a blazer or blouse the colour of which is distinct from the colours worn by the contesting teams.

(2) Referees for international matches will be selected from a neutral country unless the countries concerned agree to appoint their own officials.

(3) The referee must be chosen from the official List of International Referees. This need not apply to amateur and youth international matches.

(4) The referee shall report to the appropriate authority misconduct or any misdemeanour on the part of spectators, officials, players, named substitutes or other persons which take place either on the field of play or in its vicinity at any time prior to, during, or after the match in question so that appropriate action can be taken by the authority concerned.

(5) Assistant referees cooperate with the referee. In no case shall the referee consider the intervention of an assistant referee if he himself has seen the incident and from his position on the field, is better able to judge. With this reserve, and the assistant referee neutral, the referee can consider the intervention, and if the information of the assistant referee applies to that phase of the game immediately before the scoring of a goal, the referee may act thereon and cancel the goal.

(6) The referee, however, can only reverse his first decision so long as the game has not been restarted.

(7) If the referee applies the advantage clause and the advantage which was anticipated does not develop at that time, the referee shall penalise the original offence.

(8) The Laws of the Game are intended to provide that games should be played with as little interference as possible, and in this view it is the duty of referees to penalise only deliberate breaches of the Law. Constant whistling for trifling and doubtful breaches produces bad feeling and loss of

temper on the part of the players and spoils the pleasure of spectators.

(9) By par. (d) of Law V the referee is empowered to terminate a match in the event of grave disorder, but he has no power or right to decide, in such event, that either team is disqualified and thereby the loser of the match. He must send a detailed report to the proper authority who alone has power to deal further with this matter.

(10) If a player commits two infringements of a different nature at the same time, the referee shall punish the more serious offence.

(11) It is the duty of the referee to act upon the information of neutral assistant referees with regard to incidents that do not come under the personal notice of the referee.

(12) The referee shall not allow any person to enter the field until play has stopped, and only then if he has given him a signal to do so.

(13) A referee (or where applicable an assistant referee or fourth official) shall not be held liable for (1) any kind of injury suffered by a player, official or spectator, (2) any damage to property of any kind, or (3) any other loss suffered by any individual, club, company, association or similar body, due or which may be due to any decision which he may take in terms of the Laws of the Game or in respect of the normal procedures required to hold, play and control a match.

Such a decision may be

(a) a decision that the condition of the field of play or its surrounds or that the weather conditions are such as to allow or not to allow a match to take place,

(b) a decision to abandon a match for whatever reason,

(c) a decision as to the condition of the fixtures or equipment used during a match including the goal-posts, cross-bar, corner-posts and the ball,

(d) a decision to stop or not to stop a match due to spectator interference or any problem in the spectator area,

(e) a decision to stop or not to stop play to allow an injured player to be treated,

(f) a decision to request or insist that an injured player be removed from the field of play for treatment,

(g) a decision to allow or not to allow a player to wear certain apparel or equipment,

(h) a decision (in so far as this may be his responsibility) to allow or not to allow any persons (including team or stadium officials, security officers, photographers or other media representatives) to be present in the vicinity of the field of play,

(i) any other decision which he may take in accordance with the Laws of the Game or in conformity with his duties in terms of the Federation, Association or League Rules or Regulations under which the match is played.

(14) The coach may convey tactical instructions to players during the match.

The coach and other officials, however, must remain within the confines of the technical area*, where such an area is provided and they must conduct themselves, at all times, in a responsible manner.

(15) In tournaments or competitions where a fourth official is appointed, his role and duties shall be in accordance with the guidelines approved by the International Football Association Board.**

---

*See page 117
**See page 119

Assistant Referees

Assistant Referees

Two assistant referees shall be appointed, whose duty (subject to the decision of the referee) shall be to indicate:

(a) when the ball is out of play;

(b) which side is entitled to a corner-kick, goal-kick or throw-in;

(c) when a player may be penalised for being in an offside position;

(d) when misconduct or other incident has occurred out of the view of the referee;

(e) when a substitution is desired.

They shall also assist the referee to control the game in accordance with the Laws. In the event of undue interference or improper conduct by an assistant referee, the referee shall dispense with his services and arrange for a substitute to be appointed. (The matter shall be reported by the referee to the competent authority.)

The assistant referees should be equipped with flags by the club whose ground the match is played.

| LAW VI | **Decisions of the International F.A. Board** |

(1) Assistant referees, where neutral, shall draw the referee's attention to any breach of the Laws of the Game of which they become aware if they consider that the referee may not have seen it, but the referee shall always be the judge of the decision to be taken.

(2) In international "A" matches, national associations should appoint neutral assistant referees from the International List.

(3) In international matches assistant referee's flags shall be of a vivid colour, bright reds and yellows. Such flags are recommended for use in all other matches.

(4) An assistant referee may be subject to disciplinary action only upon a report of the referee for unjustified interference or insufficient assistance.

Duration
of the Game

Duration of the Game

The duration of the game shall be two equal periods of 45 minutes, unless otherwise mutually agreed upon, subject to the following:

(a) Allowance shall be made in either period for all time lost through substitution, the transport from the field of injured players, time-wasting or other cause, the amount of which shall be a matter for the discretion of the referee.

(b) Time shall be extended to permit a penalty-kick being taken at or after the expiration of the normal period in either half.

The half-time interval shall not exceed fifteen minutes.

Competition rules shall clearly stipulate the duration of the half-time interval.

The duration of the half-time interval may be altered only with the consent of the referee.

| LAW VII | **Decisions of the International F.A. Board** |

(1) If a match has been stopped by the referee, before the completion of the time specified in the rules, for any reason stated in Law V, it must be replayed in full unless the rules of the competition concerned provide for the result of the match at the time of such stoppage to stand.

(2) Players have a right to an interval at half-time.

The Start of Play

The Start of Play

(a) **At the beginning of the game,** choice of ends and the kick-off shall be decided by the toss of a coin. The team winning the toss shall have the option of choice of ends or the kick-off. The referee having given a signal, the game shall be started by a player taking a place-kick (i.e. a kick at the ball while it is stationary on the ground in the centre of the field of play) into his opponents' half of the field of play. Every player shall be in his own half of the field and every player of the team opposing that of the kicker shall remain not less than 10 yards from the ball until it is kicked-off; it shall not be deemed in play until it has travelled the distance of its own circumference. The kicker shall not play the ball a second time until it has been touched or played by another player.

(b) **After a goal has been scored,** the game shall be restarted in like manner by a player of the team losing the goal.

(c) After half-time; when restarting after half-time, ends shall be changed and the kick-off shall be taken by a player of the opposite team to that of the player who started the game.

Punishment:

For any infringement of this Law, the kick-off shall be retaken, except in the case of the kicker playing the ball again before it has been touched or played by another player; for this offence an indirect free-kick shall be taken by a player of the opposing team from the place where the infringement occurred, subject to the overriding conditions imposed in Law XIII.

A goal shall not be scored direct from a kick-off.

(d) After any other temporary suspension; when restarting the game after a temporary suspension of play from any cause not mentioned elsewhere in these Laws, provided that immediately prior to the suspension the ball has not passed over the touch- or goal-lines, the referee shall drop the ball at the place where it was when play was suspended, unless it was within the goal-area at that time, in which case it shall be dropped on that part of the goal-area line which runs parallel to the goal-line, at the point nearest to where the ball was when play was stopped. It shall be deemed in play when it has touched the ground; if, however, it goes over the touch- or goal-lines after it has been dropped by the referee, but before it is touched by a player, the referee shall again drop it. A player shall not play the ball until it has touched the ground.

If this section of the Laws is not complied with, the referee shall again drop the ball.

| LAW VIII | **Decisions of the International F.A. Board** |

(1) If, when the referee drops the ball, a player infringes any of the Laws before the ball has touched the ground, the player concerned shall be cautioned or sent off the field according to the seriousness of the offence, but a free-kick cannot be awarded to the opposing team because the ball was not in play at the time of the offence.

The ball shall therefore be again dropped by the referee.

(2) Kicking-off by persons other than the players competing in a match is prohibited.

Ball In
and Out of Play

Ball In and Out of Play

The ball is out of play:

(a) when it has wholly crossed the goal-line or touch-line, whether on the ground or in the air.

(b) when the game has been stopped by the referee.

The ball is in play at all other times from the start of the match to the finish including:

(a) if it rebounds from a goal-post, cross-bar or corner-flag post into the field of play.

(b) if it rebounds off either the referee or assistant referees when they are in the field of play.

(c) in the event of a supposed infringement of the Laws, until a decision is given.

Decisions of the International F.A. Board

(1) The lines belong to the areas of which they are the boundaries. In consequence, the touch-lines and the goal-lines belong to the field of play.

Method of Scoring

Method of Scoring

Except as otherwise provided by these Laws, a goal is scored when the whole of the ball has passed over the goal-line, between the goal-posts and under the cross-bar, provided it has not been thrown, carried or intentionally propelled by hand or arm, by a player of the attacking side, except in the case of a goalkeeper, who is within his own penalty-area.

The team scoring the greater number of goals during a game shall be the winner; if no goals or an equal number of goals are scored, the game shall be termed a "draw".

| LAW X | ## Decisions of the International F.A. Board

(1) Law X defines the only method according to which a match is won or drawn; no variation whatsoever can be authorised.

(2) A goal cannot in any case be allowed if the ball has been prevented by some outside agent from passing over the goal-line. If this happens in the normal course of play, other than at the taking of a penalty-kick: the game must be stopped and restarted by the referee dropping the ball at the

place where the ball came into contact with the interference, unless it was within the goal-area at that time, in which case it shall be dropped on that part of the goal-area line which runs parallel to the goal-line, at the point nearest to where the ball was when play was stopped.

(3) If, when the ball is going into goal, a spectator enters the field before it passes wholly over the goal-line and tries to prevent a score, a goal shall be allowed if the ball goes into goal unless the spectator has made contact with the ball or has interfered with play, in which case the referee shall stop the game and restart it by dropping the ball at the place where the contact or interference occurred, unless it was within the goal-area at that time, in which case it shall be dropped on that part of the goal-area line which runs parallel to the goal-line, at the point nearest to where the ball was when play was stopped.

Off-side

SOCCER

Off-side

(1) A player is in an off-side position if he is nearer to his opponents' goal-line than the ball, unless:

    (a) he is in his own half of the field of play, or

    (b) he is not nearer to his opponents' goal-line than at least two of his opponents.

(2) It is not an offence in itself to be in an off-side position

A player shall only be penalised for being in an off-side position if, at the moment the ball touches, or is played by one of his team, he is, in the opinion of the referee, involved in active play by:

    (a) interfering with play, or

    (b) interfering with an opponent, or

    (c) gaining an advantage by being in that position.

(3) A player shall not be declared off-side by the referee

(a) merely because of his being in an off-side position, or

(b) if he receives the ball direct from a goal-kick, a corner-kick or a throw-in.

(4) If a player is declared off-side, the referee shall award an indirect free-kick, which shall be taken by a player of the opposing team from the place where the infringement occurred, unless the offence is committed by a player in his opponents' goal area, in which case the free-kick shall be taken from any point within the goal area.

| LAW XI | **Decisions of the International F.A. Board** |

(1) Off-side shall not be judged at the moment the player in question receives the ball, but at the moment when the ball is passed to him by one of his own side. A player who is not in an off-side position when one of his colleagues passes the ball to him or takes a free-kick, does not therefore become off-side if he goes forward during the flight of the ball.

(2) A player who is level with the second last opponent or with the last two opponents is not in an off-side position.

Fouls and Misconduct

Fouls and Misconduct

A player who commits any of the following six offences in a manner considered by the referee to be careless, reckless or involving disproportionate force:

(a) kicks or attempts to kick an opponent; or

(b) trips an opponent; or

(c) jumps at an opponent; or

(d) charges an opponent; or

(e) strikes or attempts to strike an opponent; or

(f) pushes an opponent;

or who commits any of the following four offences:

(g) when tackling an opponent makes contact with the opponent before contact is made with the ball; or

(h) • holds an opponent; or
   • spits at an opponent; or

(i) handles the ball deliberately, i.e, carries, strikes or propels the ball with his hand or arm (this does not apply to the goalkeeper within his own penalty-area);

shall be penalised by the award of a **direct free-kick** to be taken by the opposing team from the place where the offence occurred, unless the offence is committed by a player in his opponents' goal-area, in which case the free-kick shall be taken from any point within the goal-area.

Should a player of the defending team commit one of the above ten offences within the penalty-area, he shall be penalised by a **penalty-kick.**

A penalty-kick can be awarded irrespective of the position of the ball, if in play, at the time an offence within the penalty-area is committed.

A player committing any of the five following offences:

1. Playing in a manner considered by the referee to be dangerous;

2. charging fairly, i.e. with the shoulder, when the ball is not within playing

distance of the players concerned and they are definitely not trying to play it;

3. when not playing the ball, impeding the progress of an opponent, i.e. running between the opponent and the ball, or interposing the body so as to form an obstacle to an opponent;

4. charging the goalkeeper except when he

   (a) is holding the ball;

   (b) is obstructing an opponent;

   (c) has passed outside his goal-area.

5. when playing as a goalkeeper and within his own penalty-area:

   (a) from the moment he takes control of the ball with his hands, he takes more than 4 steps in any direction whilst holding, bouncing or throwing the ball in the air and catching it again, without releasing it into play, or

   (b) having released the ball into play before, during or after the 4 steps, he touches it again with his hands, before it has been touched or played by a player of the opposing team either inside or outside of the penalty area, or by a player of the same team outside the penalty area, subject to the overriding conditions of 5(c), or

(c) touches the ball with his hands after it has been deliberately kicked to him by a team-mate, or

(d) indulges in tactics, which in the opinion of the referee, are designed to hold up the game and thus waste time and so give an unfair advantage to his own team,

shall be penalised by the award of an **indirect free-kick** to be taken by the opposing side from the place where the infringement occurred, subject to the overriding conditions imposed in Law XIII.

A player shall be **cautioned and shown the yellow card** if:

(j) he enters or re-enters the field of play to join or rejoin his team after the game has commenced, or leaves the field of play during the progress of the game (except through accident) without, in either case, first having received a signal from the referee showing him that he may do so. If the referee stops the game to administer the caution, the game shall be restarted by an indirect free-kick taken by a player of the opposing team from the place where the ball was when the referee stopped the game, subject to the overriding conditions imposed in Law XIII.

If, however, the offending player has committed a more serious offence he shall be penalised according to that section of the law he infringed.

(k) he persistently infringes the Laws of the Game;

(l) he shows, by word or action, dissent from any decision given by the referee;

(m) he is guilty of ungentlemanly conduct.

For any of these last three offences, in addition to the caution, an indirect free-kick shall also be awarded to the opposing side from the place where the offence occurred, subject to the overriding conditions imposed in Law XIII, unless a more serious infringement of the Laws of the Game was committed.

A player shall be **sent off the field of play and shown the red card,** if, in the opinion of the referee, he:

(n) is guilty of violent conduct;

(o) is guilty of serious foul play;

(p) uses foul or abusive language;

(q) is guilty of a second cautionable offence after having received a caution.

If play is stopped by reason of a player being ordered from the field for an offence without a separate breach of the Law having been committed, the game shall be resumed by an **indirect free-kick** awarded to the opposing side from the place where the infringement occurred, subject to the overriding conditions imposed in Law XIII.

| LAW XII | **Decisions of the International F.A. Board** |

(1) If the goalkeeper either strikes an opponent by throwing the ball at him or pushes him with the ball while still holding it, the referee shall award a penalty-kick, if the offence took place within the penalty-area.

(2) If a player leans on the shoulders of another player of his own team in order to head the ball, the referee shall stop the game, caution the player for ungentlemanly conduct and award an indirect free-kick to the opposing side.

(3) A player's obligation when joining or rejoining his team after the start of the match to "report to the referee" must be interpreted as meaning 'to draw the attention of the referee from the touch-line.' The signal from the referee shall be made by a definite gesture which makes the player understand that he may come into the field of play; it is not necessary for the referee to wait until the game is stopped (this does not apply in respect of an infringement of Law IV), but the referee is the sole judge of the moment in which he gives his signal of acknowledgement.

(4) The letter and spirit of Law XII do not oblige the referee to stop a game to administer a caution. He may, if he chooses, apply the advantage. If he does apply the advantage, he shall caution the player when play stops.

(5) If a player covers up the ball without touching it in an endeavour not to have it played by an opponent, he obstructs but does not infringe Law XII par. 3 because he is already in possession of the ball and covers it for tactical reasons whilst the ball remains within playing distance. In fact, he is actually playing the ball and does not commit an infringement; in this case, the player may be charged because he is in fact playing the ball.

(6) If a player positions his arms to impede an opponent and steps from one side to the other, moving his arms up and down to delay his

opponent, forcing him to change course, but does not make "bodily contact" the referee shall caution the player for ungentlemanly conduct and award an indirect free-kick.

(7) If a player impedes the progress of the opposing goalkeeper, in an attempt to prevent him from putting the ball into play in accordance with Law XII, 5 (a), the referee shall award an indirect free-kick.

(8) If, after a referee has awarded a free kick, a player protests violently by using abusive or foul language and is sent off the field, the free-kick should not be taken until the player has left the field.

(9) Any player, whether he is within or outside the field of play, whose conduct is ungentlemanly or violent, whether or not it is directed towards an opponent, a colleague, the referee, an assistant referee or other person, or who uses foul or abusive language, is guilty of an offence, and shall be dealt with according to the nature of the offence committed.

(10) If, in the opinion of the referee, a goal-keeper lies on the ball longer than is necessary, he shall be penalised for ungentlemanly conduct and

(a) be cautioned and an indirect free-kick awarded to the opposing team;

(b) in case of repetition of the offence, be sent off the field.

(11) The offence of spitting at officials and other persons, or similar unseemly behaviour shall be considered as violent conduct within the meaning of section (n) of Law XII.

(12) If, when a referee is about to caution a player, and before he has done so, the player commits another offence which merits a caution, the player shall be sent off the field of play.

(13) If, in the opinion of the referee, a player who is moving toward his opponent's goal with an obvious opportunity to score a goal is impeded by an opponent, through unlawful means, i.e. an offence punishable by a free-kick (or a penalty-kick), thus denying the attacking player's team the aforesaid goal-scoring opportunity, the offending player shall be sent off the field of play for serious foul play in accordance with Law XII (o).

(14) If, in the opinion of the referee, a player, other than the goalkeeper within his own penalty area, denies his opponents a goal, or an obvious goal-scoring opportunity, by intentionally handling the ball, he shall be sent off the field of play for serious foul play in accordance with Law XII (o).

(15) The International F.A. Board is of the opinion that a goalkeeper, in the circumstances described in Law XII 5(a), will be considered to be in control of the ball by touching it with any part of his hands or arms. Possession of the ball would include the goalkeeper intentionally parrying the ball, but would not include the circumstances where, in the opinion of the referee, the ball rebounds accidentally from the goalkeeper, for example after he has made a save.

(16) Subject to the terms of Law XII, a player may pass the ball to his own goalkeeper using his head or chest or knee, etc. If, however, in the opinion of the referee, a player uses a deliberate trick in order to circumvent article 5(c) of Law XII, the player will be guilty of ungentlemanly conduct and will be punished accordingly under the terms of Law XII; that is to say, the player will be cautioned and shown the yellow card and an indirect free-kick will be awarded to the opposing team from the place where the player committed the offence.

In such circumstances, it is irrelevant whether the goal keeper subsequently touches the ball with his hands or not. The offence is committed by the player in attempting to circumvent both the text and the spirit of Law XII.

LAW XIII

Free-kick

Free-kick

Free-kicks shall be classified under two headings: "direct" (from which a goal can be scored direct against the offending side), and "indirect" (from which a goal cannot be scored unless the ball has been played or touched by a player other than the kicker before passing through the goal).

When a player is taking a direct or an indirect free-kick inside his own penalty-area, all of the opposing players shall be at least ten yards (9.15 m) from the ball and shall remain outside the penalty-area until the ball has been kicked out of the area. The ball shall be in play immediately it has travelled the distance of its own circumference and is beyond the penalty-area. The goal-keeper shall not receive the ball into his hands, in order that he may thereafter kick it into play. If the ball is not kicked direct into play, beyond the penalty-area, the kick shall be retaken.

When a player is taking a direct or an indirect free-kick outside his own penalty-area, all of the opposing players shall be at least ten yards from the ball, until it is in play, unless they are standing on their own goal-line, between the goal-posts. The ball shall be in play when it has travelled the distance of its own circumference.

If a player of the opposing side encroaches into the penalty-area, or within ten yards of the ball, as the case may be, before a free-kick is taken, the referee shall delay the taking of the kick, until the Law is complied with.

The ball must be stationary when a free-kick is taken, and the kicker shall not play the ball a second time, until it has been touched or played by another player.

Notwithstanding any other reference in these Laws to the point from which a free-kick is to be taken:

1. Any free-kick awarded to the defending team, within its own goal-area, may be taken from any point within the goal-area.

2. Any indirect free-kick awarded to the attacking team within its opponent's goal-area shall be taken from the part of the goal-area line which runs parallel to the goal-line, at the point nearest to where the offence was committed.

Punishment:

If the kicker, after taking the free-kick, plays the ball a second time before it has been touched or played by another player, an indirect free-kick shall be taken by a player of the opposing team from the spot where the infringement occurred, unless the offence is committed by a player in his opponent's goal-area, in which case the free-kick shall be taken from any point within the goal-area.

LAW XIII | **Decisions of the International F.A. Board**

(1) In order to distinguish between a direct and an indirect free-kick, the referee, when he awards an indirect free-kick, shall indicate accordingly by raising an arm above his head. He shall keep his arm in that position until the kick has been taken and retain the signal until the ball has been played or touched by another player or goes out of play.

(2) Players who do not retire to the proper distance when a free-kick is taken must be cautioned and on any repetition be ordered off. It is particularly requested of referees that attempts to delay the taking of a free-kick by encroaching should be treated as serious misconduct.

(3) If, when a free-kick is being taken, any of the players dance about or gesticulate in a way

calculated to distract their opponents, it shall be deemed ungentlemanly conduct for which the offender(s) shall be cautioned.

Penalty-kick

Penalty-kick

A penalty-kick shall be taken from the penalty-mark and, when it is being taken, all players with the exception of the player taking the kick, properly identified, and the opposing goalkeeper, shall be within the field of play but outside the penalty-area, at least 10 yards from the penalty mark and must stand behind the penalty mark.

The opposing goalkeeper must stand (without moving his feet) on his own goal-line, between the goal-posts, until the ball is kicked. The player taking the kick must kick the ball forward; he shall not play the ball a second time until it has been touched or played by another player. The ball shall be deemed in play directly it is kicked, i.e. when it has travelled the distance of its circumference. A goal may be scored directly from a penalty-kick. When a penalty-kick is being taken during the normal course of play, or when time has been extended at half-time or full-time to allow a penalty-kick to be taken or retaken, a goal shall not be nullified if, before passing between the posts and under the cross-bar, the ball touches either or both of the goal-posts, or the cross-bar, or the goal-keeper, or any combination of these agencies, providing that no other infringement has occurred.

Punishment:

For any infringement of this Law:

(a) by the defending team, the kick shall be retaken if a goal has not resulted.

(b) by the attacking team other than by the player taking the kick, if a goal is scored it shall be disallowed and the kick retaken.

(c) by the player taking the penalty-kick, committed after the ball is in play, a player of the opposing team shall take an indirect free-kick from the spot where the infringement occurred, subject to the overriding conditions imposed in Law XIII.

LAW XIV **Decisions of the International F.A. Board**

(1) When the referee has awarded a penalty-kick, he shall not signal for it to be taken, until the players have taken up position in accordance with the Law.

(2) (a) If, after the kick has been taken, the ball is stopped in its course towards goal, by an outside agent, the kick shall be retaken.

(b) If, after the kick has been taken, the ball rebounds into play, from the goalkeeper, the cross-bar or a goal-post, and is then stopped in its course by an outside agent, the referee shall stop play and restart it by dropping the ball at the place where it came into contact with the outside agent, unless it was within the goal-area at that time, in which case it shall be dropped on that part of the goal-area line which runs parallel to the goal-line, at the point nearest to where the ball was when play was stopped.

(3) (a) If, after having given the signal for a penalty-kick to be taken, the referee sees that the goalkeeper is not in his right place on the goal-line, he shall, nevertheless, allow the kick to proceed. It shall be retaken, if a goal is not scored.

(b) If, after the referee has given the signal for a penalty-kick to be taken, and before the ball has been kicked, the goal-keeper moves his feet, the referee shall, nevertheless, allow the kick to proceed. It shall be retaken, if a goal is not scored.

(c) If, after the referee has given the signal for a penalty-kick to be taken, and before the ball is in play, a player of the defending team encroaches into the penalty-area, or within ten yards of the penalty-mark, the referee shall, nevertheless, allow the kick to proceed. It shall be retaken, if a goal is not scored.

The player concerned shall be cautioned.

(4) (a) If, when a penalty-kick is being taken, the player taking the kick is guilty of ungentlemanly conduct, the kick, if already taken, shall be retaken, if a goal is scored.

The player concerned shall be cautioned.

(b) If, after the referee has given the signal for a penalty-kick to be taken, and before the ball is in play, a colleague of the player taking the kick encroaches into the penalty-area or within ten yards of the penalty-mark, the referee shall, nevertheless, allow the kick to proceed. If a goal is scored, it shall be disallowed, and the kick retaken.

The players concerned shall be cautioned.

(c) If, in the circumstances described in the foregoing paragraph, the ball rebounds into play from the goalkeeper, the cross-bar or a goal-post, and a goal has not been scored, the referee shall stop the game, caution the player and award an indirect free-kick to the opposing team from the place where the infringement occurred, subject to the overriding conditions imposed in Law XIII.

(5) (a) If, after the referee has given the signal for a penalty-kick to be taken, and before the ball is in play, the goalkeeper moves from his position on the goal-line, or moves his feet, and a colleague of the kicker encroaches into the penalty area or within 10 yards of the penalty-mark, the kick, if taken, shall be retaken.

The colleague of the kicker shall be cautioned.

(b) If, after the referee has given the signal for a penalty-kick to be taken, and before the ball is in play, a player of each team encroaches into the penalty-area, or within 10 yards of the penalty-mark, the kick, if taken, shall be retaken.

The players concerned shall be cautioned.

(6) When a match is extended, at half-time or full-time, to allow a penalty-kick to be taken or retaken, the extension shall last until the moment that the penalty-kick has been completed, i.e. until the referee has decided whether or not a goal is scored, and the game shall terminate immediately the referee has made his decision.

After the player taking the penalty-kick has put the ball into play, no player other than the defending goalkeeper may play or touch the ball before the kick is completed.

(7) When a penalty-kick is being taken in extended time:

(a) the provisions of all of the foregoing paragraphs, except paragraphs (2)(b) and (4)(c) shall apply in the usual way, and

(b) in the circumstances described in paragraphs (2)(b) and (4)(c) the game shall terminate immediately the ball rebounds from the goalkeeper, the cross-bar or the goal-post.

Throw-in

Throw-in

When the whole of the ball passes over a touch-line, either on the ground or in the air, it shall be thrown in from the point where it crossed the line, in any direction, by a player of the team opposite to that of the player who last touched it. The thrower at the moment of delivering the ball must face the field of play and part of each foot shall be either on the touch-line or on the ground outside the touch-line. The thrower shall use both hands and shall deliver the ball from behind and over his head. The ball shall be in play immediately it enters the field of play, but the thrower shall not again play the ball until it has been touched or played by another player. A goal shall not be scored direct from a throw-in.

Punishment:

(a) If the ball is improperly thrown in the throw-in shall be taken by a player of the opposing team.

(b) If the thrower plays the ball a second time before it has been touched or played by another player, an indirect free-kick shall be taken by a player of

the opposing team from the place
where the infringement occurred,
subject to the overriding conditions
imposed in Law XIII.

| LAW XV | **Decisions of the International F.A. Board** |

(1) If a player taking a throw-in plays the ball a second
time by handling it within the field of play before it
has been touched or played by another player, the
referee shall award a direct free-kick.

(2) A player taking a throw-in must face the field of
play with some part of his body.

(3) If, when a throw-in is being taken, any of the
opposing players dance about or gesticulate in a
way calculated to distract or impede the thrower, it
shall be deemed ungentlemanly conduct, for which
the offender(s) shall be cautioned.

(4) A throw-in taken from any position other than the
point where the ball passed over the touch-line
shall be considered to have been improperly thrown
in.

Goal-kick

SOCCER

Goal-kick

When the whole of the ball passes over the goal-line excluding that portion between the goal-posts, either in the air or on the ground, having last been played by one of the attacking team, it shall be kicked direct into play beyond the penalty-area from any point within the goal-area by a player of the defending team. A goalkeeper shall not receive the ball into his hands from a goal-kick in order that he may thereafter kick it into play. If the ball is not kicked beyond the penalty-area, i.e. direct into play, the kick shall be retaken. The kicker shall not play the ball a second time until it has touched or been played by another player. A goal shall not be scored direct from such a kick. Players of the team opposing that of the player taking the goal-kick shall remain outside the penalty-area until the ball has been kicked out of the penalty-area.

Punishment:

If a player taking a goal-kick plays the ball a second time after it has passed beyond the penalty area, but before it has touched or been played by another player, an indirect free-kick shall be awarded to the opposing team, to be taken from the place where the infringement occurred, subject to the overriding conditions imposed in Law XIII.

| LAW XVI | **Decisions of the International F.A. Board** |

(1) When a goal-kick has been taken and the player who has kicked the ball touches it again before it has left the penalty-area, the kick has not been taken in accordance with the Law and must be retaken.

Corner-kick

Corner-kick

When the whole of the ball passes over the goal-line, excluding that portion between the goal-posts, either in the air or on the ground, having last been played by one of the defending team, a member of the attacking team shall take a corner-kick, i.e. the whole of the ball shall be placed within the quarter circle at the nearest corner-flagpost, which must not be moved, and it shall be kicked from that position. A goal may be scored direct from such a kick. Players of the team opposing that of the player taking the corner-kick shall not approach within 10 yards of the ball until it is in play, i.e. it has travelled the distance of its own circumference, nor shall the kicker play the ball a second time until it has been touched or played by another player.

Punishment:

(a) If the player who takes the kick plays the ball a second time before it has been touched or played by another player, the referee shall award an indirect free-kick to the opposing team, to be taken from the place where the infringement occurred, subject to the overriding conditions imposed in Law XIII.

(b) For any other infringement the kick shall be retaken.

Appendix

Additional Instructions Regarding the Laws of the Game

The following decisions and instructions to referees conform with the Laws of the Game and the decisions of the International F.A. Board. They are therefore regarded as authoritative and quoted as such.

1. **Serious foul play and violent conduct**

   Football being a tough, combative sport— where the contest to gain possession of the ball should nonetheless be fair and gentlemanly—any such moves, even when really vigorous, must be allowed by the referee.

   Serious foul play and violent conduct are, however, strictly forbidden and the referee must react to them by stringently applying the Laws of the Game.

   These two offences can be defined as follows:

   (a) it is *serious foul play* when a player infringes the Laws of the Game and uses intentional violence when challenging for the ball against an opponent.

(b) it is *violent conduct* when a player is guilty of aggression towards an opponent even when they are not challenging for the ball. The ball can be in or out of play. If the ball is in play he shall be sanctioned with a direct free kick in favour of the team of the player who was attacked, from the place where the offence was committed, or with a penalty kick if it took place within the penalty area. If the ball is out of play, the game shall be resumed at the stage where it was interrupted prior to the offence (throw-in, free kick, etc.). Moreover, if a player attacks one of his teammates, the referee, an assistant referee, a spectator etc., this shall also be considered violent conduct. As mentioned above, this offence can arise when the ball is in or out of play. If the ball is in play, the player shall be sanctioned with an indirect free kick against his team from the spot where the violent conduct occurred or with a dropped ball taken at the place where the ball was situated at the time of the offence, if this occurred beyond the boundaries of the field of play. If the ball is out of play the game shall be resumed at the stage where it was interrupted prior to the offence (throw-in, free kick, etc.).

2. Tackling

(a) *A sliding tackle* with one or both legs is permissible if, in the opinion of the referee, it is not dangerous. If, however, the player making the tackle, instead of making contact with the ball, trips his opponent, the referee shall award a direct free kick to the opposing team and shall *caution* the offending player.

(b) *A tackle from behind* which is violent with little or no attempt to play the ball is prohibited and will be punished by a **direct free kick <u>and</u> an ordering off.**

3. Offences against goalkeepers

It is an offence if a player:

(a) jumps at a goalkeeper under the pretext of heading the ball;

(b) dodges about in front of a goalkeeper in order to prevent him from releasing the ball;

(c) who is standing in front of a goalkeeper when a corner kick is being taken, takes advantage of his position to obstruct the goalkeeper before the kick is taken and before the ball is in play;

(d) attempts to kick the ball when the goalkeeper is in the process of releasing it.

4. Obstruction

A player who has the ball under control within playing distance (i.e. the distance at which the player is covering the ball for tactical reasons in order to avoid its being played by an opponent, without using his arms) is not guilty of obstruction.

Any player who intentionally obstructs an opponent by crossing directly in front of him or running between him and the ball or intervening so as to form an obstacle with the aim of delaying his advance, must be sanctioned with an indirect free kick in favour of the opposing team.

However, any player who intentionally impedes the progress of an opponent by physical contact, whether using his hand, arm, leg or any other part of his body, shall be penalised by the award of a direct free kick to the opposing team, or by a penalty kick, if the offence was committed within his penalty area.

5. Scissors or bicycle kick

Such a kick is permissible, provided that in the opinion of the referee it is not dangerous to an opponent.

6. Jumping at an opponent

A player who jumps at an opponent under the pretext of heading the ball, shall be penalised by the award of a direct free kick to the opposing team.

7. Prohibited use of body

A player who holds off an opponent using his hand, arm, leg or body, is guilty of an infringement of Law XII and shall be punished by the award of a direct free kick to the opposing team.

Holding or hindering an opponent when the ball is out of play in order to prevent him from running into position is an offence (disciplinary punishment).

8. Caution for handling the ball or holding an opponent

Whilst it is not usual for a player to be cautioned for handling the ball or holding an opponent, there are exceptional circumstances in which, in addition to imposing the customary punishment, the referee must caution a player for ungentlemanly conduct in these offences:

(a) when a player, in order to prevent an opponent from gaining possession of the ball, and because he is unable to play it in any other way, stops it with one, or both hands, punches it or catches it, or

(b) when a player holds an opponent in order to prevent him from gaining possession of the ball.

(c) when an attacking player attempts to score a goal by illegal use of the hand.

<u>The foregoing is subject to the provisions contained in decision 14 of Law XII of the International F.A. Board. (obvious goal or goal-scoring opportunity denied = ordering offence).</u>

9. **Free kicks**

   (a) The referee shall indicate the award of an indirect free kick by raising an arm above his head. He shall keep his arm in that position until the kick has been taken and the ball has been played or touched by another player or goes out of play.

(b) Any player who, for any reason, deliberately delays a free kick being taken by the opposing team shall be cautioned (yellow card). For repetition of this offence he shall be sent off (red card).

(c) Any player who prematurely rushes forward from the defensive wall, formed at least 10 yards (9.15 m) from the ball, before the ball has been kicked, shall be cautioned. In the event of repetition of this offence, he shall be sent off.

While the Law states that all opposing players should retire to a distance of at least 10 yards (9.15 m) from the ball, the referee has discretionary power to disregard this requirement to enable a free kick to be taken quickly.

10. Penalty kick

(a) *Conduct during a penalty kick*

During a penalty kick, the goalkeeper shall stand on the goal-line without moving his feet. Apart from the goalkeeper and the player taking the kick, all the players shall take up position outside the penalty area at least 10 yards (9.15 m) away from the penalty mark and stay there until the kick has been taken.

Any breach of these conditions shall be dealt with in accordance with Law XIV.

(b) *Penalty kick at the end of the first half or at the end of the match*

If play is prolonged before half-time or at the end of the match to allow for a penalty kick to be taken or for one to be retaken, a goal shall not be disallowed if, before passing the goalposts under the crossbar, the ball touches one of the two goalposts or the crossbar or goalkeeper, or a combination of these, providing no infringement has been committed.

11. Player in offside position

(a) <u>It is not an offence in itself to be in an offside position.</u>

(b) A player shall be penalised for being offside, if, at the moment the ball touches, or is played by, one of his team, he is, in the opinion of the referee <u>involved in the active play</u> by

  1. interfering with play or with an opponent, or

    2. seeking to gain an advantage by being in that position.

(c) A player shall not be declared offside by the referee

    1. merely because of his being in an offside position, or

    2. if he receives the ball directly from a goal-kick, a corner kick or a throw-in.

    An assistant referee should not signal merely because a player is in an offside position.

12. Goalkeepers

The following principles shall apply:

A goalkeeper who is within his own penalty area:

(a) from the moment he takes control of the ball with his hands, takes <u>more than 4 steps</u> in any direction whilst holding, bouncing or throwing the ball in the air and catching it again, without releasing it into play, or, having released the ball into play before, during or after the 4 steps, he touches it again with his hands, before it has been touched or played by another player of the same team outside of the penalty area, or by a player of the opposing team either inside or outside of the penalty area subject to the overriding conditions of Law XII, 5(c), or

(b) indulges in tactics which, in the opinion of the referee, are designed merely to hold up the game and thus waste time and so give an unfair advantage to his own team, shall be penalised by the award of an indirect free kick to be taken by the opposing team from the place where the infringement occurred.

Furthermore, <u>attention must be paid to the contents of decision 15 of Law XII of the International F.A. Board.</u>

13. Persistent Infringements

Any player who persistently infringes the Laws of the Game shall be cautioned.

14. Player sent off after receiving two cautions

If a player is sent off for committing a second cautionable offence, the referee shall first show the yellow card followed immediately by the red card (so that it is obvious that the player is being sent off for the second cautionable offence and not for an offence requiring immediate expulsion).

15. Substitution

A player who is going to be replaced may not leave the field of play without the referee's permission and then only when the ball is out of play.

The substitute may then enter the field at the halfway line only.

16. Injury of a player

Team officials are permitted to enter the field of play with the referee's permission solely for the purpose of assessing an injury—not to treat it—and to arrange for the player's removal.

17. Attitude towards referees

Any player who protests at a referee's decision shall be cautioned. Any player who assaults or insults a referee shall be sent off. The captain of a team, although responsible for his team's behaviour, has no special rights.

18. Throw-in

A throw-in may not be taken from a distance of more than one metre outside the touch-line. Players are forbidden from standing directly in front of the footballer who is taking the throw-in so as to harass him.

19. Wasting time

<u>Any player who wastes time shall be cautioned for ungentlemanly conduct.</u>

Wasting time occurs whenever:

(a) a player:

* feigns injury;

* takes a free kick from a wrong position with the sole intention of forcing the referee to demand a retake;

* appears to prepare for a throw-in but suddenly leaves it to one of his team to throw in;

* kicks the ball away or carries it away with the hands after the referee has stopped play for any reason;

* stands in front of the ball when a free kick has been awarded to the opposing

team in order to give his team time to organise the defensive wall;

- excessively delays taking a throw-in or a free kick;

- delays leaving the field when being substituted.

(b) a goalkeeper:

- employs all manner of tactics with the sole intention of gaining time for his team (keeping the ball longer than necessary, waiting too long before passing it into play etc.).

20. Celebration of goal

After a goal has been scored, the player who has scored it is allowed to share his joy with his team-mates. However, the referee must not allow them to spend an inordinate amount of time in their opponents' half of the field. Neither will he tolerate players dashing past the billboards or climbing up the crowd barriers. In either of these last two cases, he will <u>caution the offending player for ungentlemanly conduct.</u>

21. Liquid refreshments during the match

Players shall be entitled to take liquid refreshments during a stoppage in the match but only on the touchline. It is forbidden to throw plastic water bags or any other water containers onto the field.

22. Inspection of studs

The referee, in co-operation with his assistant referees, shall inspect the players' studs in the corridor leading from the dressing rooms to the fields, as they are about to go on to the field for the start of the match.

23. Players' outfits

(a) The referee shall ensure that each player wears his clothes properly and check that they conform with the requirements of Law IV. Players shall be made aware that their jersey remains tucked inside their shorts and that their socks remain pulled up. The referee shall also make sure that each player is wearing shinguards and that none of them is wearing potentially dangerous objects (such as watches, metal bracelets etc.).

(b) Players are permitted to wear visible undergarments such as thermopants. They must, however, be the same colour as the shorts of the team of the player wearing them and not extend beyond the top of the knee. If a team wears multicoloured shorts, the undergarment must be the same colour as the predominant colour.

Instructions Regarding the Taking of Kicks from the Penalty Marks

(In knock-out competition to decide the winner)

Conditions under which kicks from the penalty mark shall be taken to determine which of the two teams in a drawn match, in a knock-out competition, shall be declared the winner.

(To replace drawing lots)

The International Board at its meeting on 27 June 1970 accepted a proposal by the Fédération Internationale de Football Association that the practice of drawing lots to determine which of two teams in a drawn match should proceed to a later stage of a knock-out competition or receive the trophy (if any) be discontinued and be replaced by the taking of kicks from the penalty mark which shall not be considered part of the match, subject to the following conditions:

1. The referee shall choose the goal at which all of the kicks shall be taken.

2. He shall toss a coin, and the team whose captain wins the toss shall take the first kick.

3. The referee shall note each player as he takes a kick from the penalty mark.

4. **(a)** Subject to the terms of the following paragraphs (c) and (d) both teams shall take five kicks.

   (b) The kicks shall be taken alternately.

   (c) If, before both teams have taken five kicks, one has scored more goals than the other could, even if it were to complete its five kicks, the taking of kicks shall cease.

   (d) If, after both teams have taken five kicks, both have scored the same number of goals or have not scored any goals, the taking of kicks shall continue, in the same order, until such time as both have taken an equal number of kicks (not necessarily five more kicks) and one has scored a goal more than the other.

5. The team which scores the greater number of goals, whether the number of kicks taken is in accordance with the terms of the foregoing paragraph 4(a),

4(c) or 4(d) shall qualify for the next round of the competition, or shall be declared winner of the competition, as the case may be.

6. **(a)** With the exception referred to in the following paragraph (b) only the players who are on the field of play at the end of the match, which shall mean at the end of extra time in so far as a match in which extra time is authorised is concerned, and any who, having left the field temporarily with or without the referee's permission, are not on the field of play at that time, shall take part in the taking of the kicks.

    (b) Provided that his team has not already made use of the maximum number of substitutes permitted by the rules of the competition under which the match is played, a goalkeeper who sustains an injury during the taking of the kicks and who, because of the injury, is unable to continue as goalkeeper, may be replaced by a substitute.

7. Each kick shall be taken by a different player, and not until all eligible players of any team, including the goalkeeper or the

named substitute by whom he was replaced under the terms of paragraph 6 as the case may be, have each taken a kick, may a player of the same team take a second kick.

8. Subject to the terms of paragraph 6, any player who is eligible may change places with his goalkeeper at any time during the taking of the kicks.

9. (a) Other than the player taking a kick from the penalty mark, and the two goal-keepers, all players shall remain within the centre circle whilst the taking of kicks is in progress.

   (b) The goalkeeper who is a colleague of the kicker, shall take up position within the field of play, outside the penalty area at which the kicks are being taken, behind the line which runs parallel with the goal-line, and at least 10 yards from the penalty mark.

   (c) The goalkeeper is reminded that he must remain on the goal-line between the posts until the ball is kicked into play.

10. Unless stated to the contrary in the foregoing paragraphs 1 to 9, the Laws of

the Game, and the International Board Decisions relating thereto, shall, in so far as they can, apply at the taking of the kicks.

N.B.:

In the event of light failing before the end of the taking of kicks from the penalty mark, the result shall be decided by the toss of a coin or drawing lots.

Taking of Kicks from the Penalty Marks Checklist for Referees

1. Decide at which end the kicks will be taken. This can be an important decision if the supporters of one team are behind one goal and those of the other team are at the opposite goal.

2. The team which wins the toss must take the first kick.

3. Before the kicks begin, ensure that all team officials, etc., have left the field and that only the players are left.

4. Make sure all players, apart from the kicker and the two goalkeepers are inside the centre circle.

5. Make sure the goalkeeper of the kicker's team stands outside the penalty area, in the position shown in the diagram.

6. The Laws of the Game, particularly Law XIV "The Penalty Kick," apply except where modified by the instructions for the taking of kicks from the penalty mark. Be particularly vigilant therefore for instances of gamesmanship or for

infringements by the goalkeeper, e.g. moving before the ball is kicked.

7. Keep a careful record of the kicks taken.

8. Where you have the co-operation of neutral assistant referees some of those duties may be taken by them, e.g. one assistant referee at the centre circle would organise players coming to take the kick while the other would assist by indicating whether or not the ball has crossed the goal-line.

9. It is very important that the referee organises the taking of kicks from the penalty mark correctly. Make sure you fully understand the instructions.

10. The taking of kicks from the penalty mark never forms part of an actual match. It is only a method of deciding a winner.

11. If, at the taking of kicks from the penalty mark, the light fails badly and the kicks therefore cannot be completed, the result shall be decided by tossing a coin or drawing lots.

12. An injured player may be excused from the taking of kicks from the penalty mark.

13. It is the responsibility of each team to select the players who will take the kicks

from the penalty mark. The referee's only duty is to ensure that they are taken correctly.

14. When all the players in a team have taken a kick from the penalty mark, it is not necessary that they follow the same order in taking their second kick as they had for the first series of kicks.

15. If a player who has already been cautioned commits a second cautionable offence at the taking of kicks from the penalty mark, he shall be sent off.

16. If the lights fail at a stadium after extra time but before the taking of kicks from the penalty mark, and they cannot be repaired in a reasonable time, the referee shall decide the match by tossing a coin or drawing lots.

17. A substitute who has not taken part in the match, including extra time where it is played, may not take part in kicks from the penalty mark, except to replace an injured goalkeeper.

18. After each team has taken 10 kicks from the penalty mark, a team which has had a player sent off may use a player who has already taken a kick for the 11th kick.

19. If at the end of the match some players leave the field of play and fail to return for the taking of kicks from the penalty mark, and are not injured, the referee shall not allow the kicks to be taken and shall report the matter to the responsible authorities.

20. If, at the taking of kicks from the penalty mark, or when extended time is being allowed for a penalty-kick to be taken in normal playing time, the ball strikes the goalpost or crossbar, strikes the goalkeeper and enters the goal, a goal shall be awarded.

THE TAKING OF KICKS FROM THE PENALTY MARK

No officials, coaches, etc. allowed on field of play

Referee

Assistant referee

All other players within Centre Circle

Kicker

Goalkeeper of kicker's team

Assistant referee

FAIRPLAY

FAIR PLAY

The Technical Area

The technical area as defined in Law V, International F.A. Board Decision no. 14, relates particularly to matches played in stadia with a designated seated area for technical staff and substitutes as shown below.

It is recognised that technical areas may vary between stadia, for example in size or location, but notwithstanding, the following notes are issued for general guidance.

1. The technical area shall be considered as extending 1 metre on either side of the designated seated area and shall extend forward up to a distance of 1 metre away from the touchline.

2. It is recommended that markings be used to define this area.

3. The number of persons permitted to occupy the technical area shall be defined by the rules of the competition.

4. The occupants of the technical area shall be identified before the commencement of the match in accordance with the rules of the competition.

5. Only one person has the authority to convey tactical instructions and he must return to his position immediately after giving these instructions.

6. The coach and other officials must remain within the confines of the technical area except in special circumstances, for example, a physio or doctor entering the field of play with the referee's permission to treat an injured player.

7. The coach and other occupants of the technical area must conduct themselves, at all times, in a responsible manner.

The Role of the Fourth Official

1. He may be appointed under the rules of a competition and shall officiate in the event of any of the three match officials being unable to continue.

2. The organiser, prior to the start of the competition, shall state clearly whether, in the event of any referee being unable to continue, the fourth official would take over as the match referee or whether the senior assistant referee would take over as referee with the fourth official becoming an assistant referee.

3. The fourth official shall assist with any administrative duties before, during and after the match as required by the referee.

4. He shall be responsible for assisting with substitution procedures during the match.

5. He shall supervise the replacement footballs where required. If during a match the match ball has to be replaced he shall, on the instructions of the referee,

provide another ball thus keeping the delay to a minimun.

6. He shall have the authority to check the equipment of substitutes prior to their entering the field of play. In the event of their equipment not being within the Laws of the Game he shall inform the assistant referee who shall then inform the referee.

7. The fourth official will assist the referee at all times.

8. After the match the fourth official will submit a report to the appropriate authorities, on any misconduct or other incident which has occurred out of the vision of the referee and the assistant referees. The fourth official must advise the referee and his assistants of any report being made.

Diagrams Illustrating Off-Side

Note: The players marked ⊗ are attacking the goal and the players marked ○ are defending.

Direction of movement of ball:

– – – – – – – – – – – – – – – – ➤

Direction of movement of player:

―――――――――――➤

Diagram 1 - Off-Side

OFFSIDE

Pass to a Team Mate

A passes the ball to **B**.

B is **off-side** because he is in front of **A** and is nearer to his opponents' goal-line than at least two opponents when the ball was passed by **A**.

Diagram 2 - Off-Side

Pass to a Team Mate

A plays the ball forward to **B** who is **level** with the second last defender.

B is **not off-side** since, **at the moment the ball was played by A,** he was not nearer to his opponents' goal-line than at least two opponents.

Diagram 3 - Off-Side

Pass to a Team Mate

A plays the ball forward to **B** who is **level** with the second last defender.

B is **not off-side** since, **at the moment the ball was played by A,** he was not nearer to his opponents' goal-line than at least two of his opponents.

Player **C**, lying injured outside the penalty area **is in an off-side position** but would **not be penalised** since he is not involved in **active play.**

Diagram 4 - Off-Side

Pass to a Team Mate

A plays the ball to **B** who is **level** with the last two opponents.

B is not off-side since, **at the moment the ball was played by A,** he was not nearer his opponents' goal-line than at least two of his opponents.

Diagram 5 - Off-Side

Pass to a Team Mate

A crosses the ball forward from outside the penalty area.

B runs from Position 1 and collects the ball as it lands at Position 2.

B is **off-side** since, **at the moment the ball was played by A,** he was nearer to his opponents' goal-line than at least two of his opponents and **gained an advantage** by being **in active play.**

Diagram 6 - Off-Side

NOT OFFSIDE

Pass to a Team Mate

A passes the ball to **B** who runs from
Position 1 to Position 2 to play it.

B is **not off-side** because **at the
moment the ball was played by A,** he
was **not in an off-side position** since he
was not in front of the ball and was not
nearer to his opponents' goal-line than at
least two of his opponents.

Diagram 7 - Off-Side

Inter-passing with a Team Mate

A plays the ball to **B** from Position 1 and runs forward to receive the return pass.

B plays the ball to **A** who is now in Position 2.

A is **off-side** since **at the moment the ball was played forward to him by B,** he was nearer his opponents' goal line than at least two of his opponents and **gained an advantage** by being in **active play.**

Diagram 8 - Off-Side

Interfering with an Opponent

A shoots for goal and the ball enters the net.

B is standing in front of the goalkeeper.

The goal would not be allowed since **B**, who is in an **off-side** position, is **involved in active play** and is **interfering with an opponent.**

Diagram 9 - Off-Side

Shot at Goal

A shoots for goal and scores.

Although **B** is in an off-side position, he is **not** involved in **active play** and the goal **would be allowed**.

Diagram 10 - Off-Side

Ball Rebounding from Goal Posts or Crossbar

A shoots for goal and the ball rebounds from the post to **B** who kicks the ball into the goal.

The goal would be disallowed since **B,** who was in an **off-side** position when the ball was last played by **A,** was in **active play** and **gained an advantage** by being in that position.

Diagram 11 - Off-Side

Shot Rebounds from Goalkeeper

A shoots the ball at goal and the ball rebounds from the goalkeeper to player **B**.

The goal is disallowed since **B**, who was in an **off-side** position when the ball was last played by **A**, was in **active play** and **gained an advantage** by being in that position.

Diagram 12 - Off-Side

Ball Rebounding from Goal Posts or Crossbar

A shoots for goal and the ball rebounds from the post to **B** who kicks the ball into goal.

The goal is disallowed since **B,** who was in an **off-side** position when the ball was last played by **A,** was in **active play** and **gained an advantage** by being in that position.

Diagram 13 - Off-Side

Not Interfering with an Opponent

A shoots for goal and scores.

Although **B** is lying injured in an **off-side** position, he is **not involved in active play.**

The goal would be allowed.

Diagram 14 - Off-Side

Interfering with an Opponent

A shoots for goal and the ball enters the net.

B, who is lying injured in the goal area and in the path of the ball, would be **penalised for off-side.** By his presence, however accidental, he is **involved in the active play** and **is interfering with an opponent.**

Diagram 15 - Off-Side

Corner Kick

A takes a corner kick and the ball goes to **B**.

B shoots for goal and the ball is touched by **C** and enters the goal. The goal is not permitted since **C** was in front of the ball and there was not at least two opponents between him and the goal-line when it was last played by **B**.

Diagram 16 - Off-Side

Corner Kick

A corner kick is taken by **A** and the ball goes to **B** who scores.

Although **B** has only one opponent between him and the goal-line, **the goal is allowed** since a player cannot be off-side if he received the ball direct from a corner kick.

Diagram 17 - Off-Side

NOT OFFSIDE

ЧЕСТНАЯ ИГРА
ПОЖАЛУЙСТА

請公平競爭

Throw-in

A throws the ball to **B** who scores.

The goal is allowed.

Although **B** is in front of the ball and there is only one opponent between him and the goal-line, he is **not off-side** because a player cannot be off-side if he receives the ball direct from a throw-in.

Diagram 18 - Off-Side

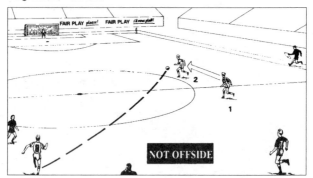

Pass to a Team Mate

B plays the ball ahead of **A** who is in his own half.

Although there are not at least two opponents nearer their own goal-line at the moment when **B** played the ball, **A** is **not off-side** since a player cannot be off-side in his own half of the field of play.

Diagram 19a - Off-Side

The ball is kicked to the goalkeeper by defender **X.**

An attacking player **A** runs towards the goalkeeper to challenge him.

Diagram 19b - Off-Side

The goalkeeper kicks the ball up-field and the attacking player **A** turns to take up an onside position.

Diagram 19c - Off-Side

The ball is intercepted by player **B,** a team-mate of the attacking player. It is transferred to another team-mate, player **C,** on the wing.

Although the attacking player **A** is in an **off-side** position, he **would not be penalised** since he is not involved in **active play.**

Diagrams Illustrating Serious Foul Play

Diagram 1 - Serious Foul Play

The attacker, number 9, is making his way towards goal with an obvious goalscoring opportunity when he is tripped by a defender.

According to Law XII, Decision 13, this **is** regarded as serious foul play and the defender must be sent off.

Diagram 2 - Serious Foul Play

An attacker is making his way towards goal when he is tripped by an opponent. He does not, however, have an obvious goalscoring opportunity.

According to Law XII, Decision 13, this **is not** regarded as serious foul play.

Diagram 3 - Serious Foul Play

FIFA FAIR PLAY

An attacker making his way to goal with an obvious goalscoring opportunity attempts to move past the goalkeeper who (intentionally) holds him. A penalty kick is awarded.

According to Law XII, Decision 13, this **is** regarded as serious foul play and the goalkeeper must be sent off.

Diagram 4 - Serious Foul Play

FIFA FAIR PLAY

An attacker is held by the goalkeeper inside the penalty area and a penalty kick is awarded. The attacker is moving away from goal and so does not have an obvious goalscoring opportunity.

According to Law XII, Decision 13, this **is not** regarded as serious foul play.

Diagram 5 - Serious Foul Play

FIFA FAIR PLAY

The attacker is tripped inside the penalty area and a penalty kick is awarded. There is, however, no obvious goalscoring opportunity since the player is moving away from goal.

According to Law XII, Decision 13, this **is not** regarded as serious foul play.

Diagram 6 - Serious Foul Play

The attacker, number 11, is tripped but
there is no obvious goalscoring
opportunity since he is not moving
towards goal.

According to Law XII, Decision 13, this **is
not** regarded as serious foul play.

Diagram 7 - Serious Foul Play

An attacker shoots for goal but an outfield player punches the ball over the bar, thus preventing a goal being scored.

According to Law XII, Decision 14, this player **is guilty of serious foul play** and must be sent off.

If the defender had intentionally punched or handled the ball and had entered the goal, he would not have been guilty of serious foul play according to Law XII, Decision 14, but he should be cautioned for ungentlemanly conduct.

Diagram 8 - Serious Foul Play

FIFA FAIR PLAY

An attacker, number 10, plays the ball and it is handled by a defender inside the penalty area. A penalty kick is awarded.

According to Law XII, Decision 14, this **is not** regarded as serious foul play.

If the ball had struck the defender on the hand accidentally, no offence would have been committed and play would have been allowed to continue.

Diagram 9 - Serious Foul Play

The attacker, number 11, is running on to a forward pass and has an obvious goalscoring opportunity. A defender jumps up and deliberately handles the ball thus preventing an obvious goalscoring opportunity.

According to Law XII, Decision 14, this player **is guilty of serious foul play** and must be sent off.

Diagram 10 - Serious Foul Play

FIFA FAIR PLAY

An attacker is running on to a forward pass with an obvious goalscoring opportunity when the goalkeeper rushes from his goal and handles the ball outside the penalty area.

According to Law XI, Decision 14, the goalkeeper **is guilty of serious foul play** and must be sent off.

Co-operation Between the Referee and Assistant Referees—Law VI

In the Laws of the Game set out in the foregoing pages there are no instructions as to the relative positioning of the referee and assistant referees during a game. There are, however, instructions in Laws V and VI with regard to the powers and duties of the referee and assistant referee which, rightly interpreted, imply co-operation. Law VI stipulates that two assistant referees shall be appointed, whose duty (subject to the decision of the referee) shall be to:

(a) signal when the ball is out of play;

(b) signal when the ball has crossed the goal-line and whether a corner-kick or a goal-kick is to be awarded;

(c) signal which side is entitled to the throw-in;

(d) assist the referee in conducting the game in accordance with the Laws.

The assistance referred to in (d) consists of:

1. signalling when the whole of the ball is out of play;

2. indicating which side is entitled to the corner-kick, the goal-kick, or the throw-in;

3. calling the attention of the referee to rough play or ungentlemanly conduct;

4. indicating to the referee when a substitution is desired;

5. giving an opinion on any point on which the referee may consult him.

Neutral assistant referees

The assistance referred to above is best given by neutral assistant referees. A limitation is placed upon club assistant referees because points 2., 3. and 4. are not usually referred to assistant referees who are not neutral. Neutral assistant referees must co-operate with the referee. In this case, the referee must adopt the appropriate attitude, because in effect there are three officials supervising play; the referee as principal official and the assistant referees to help him to control the game in a proper manner.

Club assistant referees

To acquire the most effective co-operation from club assistant referee, the following procedure shall be adopted:

1. Both club assistant referees shall report to the referee before the start of the match for instructions. He shall inform them that, regardless of their personal opinion, his decision is final and must not be questioned.

2. Their work as club assistant referees is to signal when the ball is entirely over the touch-line and to indicate which side is entitled to the throw-in, subject always to the decision of the referee.

   Keeping in mind their distinct duties as outlined above, the referee shall decide beforehand exactly what he requires of the club assistant referees and, as head of the trio, tell them clearly how they can best assist him. The three officials must therefore confer before the match and the referee's instructions must be specific in order to avoid confusion. The assistant referees must, for their part, fully appreciate the referee's supreme authority and accept his rulings without question should there be any difference of opinion amongst them.

They must be supportive and never contradict his decisions.

The referee shall use the diagonal system of control if his assistant referees are neutral. If they are not neutral, he shall inform them which method he intends to use. He shall co-operate with his assistant referees on the following matters and tell them:

(a) the time by his watch;

(b) the side of the field which each assistant referee shall take in each half of the match;

(c) their duties prior to the start of the game, such as checking the appurtenances on the field;

(d) who shall be the senior assistant referee, if need be;

(e) their positioning during corner-kicks;

(f) the sign denoting that he has noticed his assistant referee's signal but has overruled it;

(g) which detail in the throw-in shall be observed by the assistant referee and which by the referee. Some referees ask their assistant referees to watch out for foot faults while they

themselves concentrate on hand
faults.

Referees must not necessarily keep to one
diagonal of the field of play. If the state of
the ground or the weather demands a
switch to the opposite diagonal, the
referee shall indicate his intention to
make such a change-over to the assistant
referees, who shall immediately move to
the other half of their line. One advantage
of such a change in diagonal is that the
surface of the ground next to the touch-
line will be less worn out because the
whole length of the field will be utilised.

Other methods of co-operation may be
used as long as all three officials are aware
of them.

Signals by Referee and Assistant Referees

The signals illustrated in this booklet have been approved by the International F.A. Board for use by registered referees of affiliated national associations.

Illustrations concerning signals by the referee are shown on pages 94–97. They are simple, universally in use, and well understood.

While it is not the duty of the referee to explain or mime any offence that has caused him to give a particular decision, there are times when a simple gesture or word of guidance can aid communication and contribute to greater understanding and more respect, to the mutual benefit of referee and players. Improving communication should be encouraged, but the exaggerated miming of offences can be undignified and confusing and should not be used.

An indication by the referee of the point where a throw-in should be taken may well help prevent a player from taking a throw-in improperly. A call of "Play on, advantage" confirms to a player that the referee has not simply missed a foul, but has chosen to apply advantage. Even an indication that the ball was minutely deflected by its touching another player on its path across a touch-line might be helpful too in generating a greater understanding between referee and players. A better understanding will lead to more harmonious relationships.

All signals given by the referee should be simple, clear and instinctive. They should be designed to control the game efficiently and to ensure continuous play as far as possible; they are intended essentially to indicate what the next action in the game should be, not principally to justify that action.

An arm pointing to indicate a corner-kick, goal-kick or foul, and the direction in which it is to be taken, will normally be sufficient. The raised arm to indicate that a free-kick is indirect is clearly understood, but if a player queries politely whether the award is a direct free-kick or an indirect free-kick, a helpful word from the referee, in addition to the appropriate signal, will lead to a better understanding in future.

The duties of the referee and assistant referees are set out briefly but clearly in the Laws of the Game, Laws V and VI.

The proper use of the whistle, voice and hand signals by the referee and the flags by the assistant referees should all assist understanding through clear communication.

Co-operation between Assistant Referees and Referee

When play has been stopped, the assistant referee shall assist the referee by signalling in the following manner for the following incidents:

1. **Off-side.** The assistant referee shall lower his flag at full arm's length to the positions illustrated, and point across the field of play to indicate the spot from which the kick shall be taken. The only exception would be where the referee has decided to position himself to judge off-side when play develops from a corner-kick, penalty-kick or free-kick close to goal.

2. **Throw-in.** When the ball goes out of play over the touch-line on his side of the field, the assistant referee shall indicate the direction of the throw. He shall also signal if the thrower's feet, at the moment of release of the ball, are incorrectly placed.

3. **Corner- and goal-kicks.** When the
    whole of the ball goes out of play over the
    goal-line the assistant referee shall
    indicate whether a corner-kick or goal-
    kick shall be given.

4. **Goal.** When the referee indicates that a
    goal has been scored the assistant referee
    shall return quickly to his position
    towards the half-way line.

5. **Substitution.** When a substitution is to
    be made, the assistant referee nearest to
    the point of substitution shall attract the
    attention of the referee by illustration
    included in "Signals by the Assistant
    Referees" on page 168.

    Law XII. If the assistant referee senses
    that the referee has not seen an
    infringment, he shall raise his flag high.
    If the referee stops play, assistant referee
    shall indicate diection of the free-kick
    (direct or indirect), otherwise he shall
    lower his flag.

    (Illustrations of signals by the assistant
    referees see pages 168–176.)

Signals by the Referee

Play On - Advantage

Where the referee sees an offence but uses the "advantage," he shall indicate that play shall continue.

Penalty-Kick

The referee clearly indicates the penalty-mark, but there is no need to run towards it.

Indirect Free-kick

This signal shall be maintained until the kick has been taken and retained until the ball has been played or touched by another player or goes out of play.

Direct Free-kick
The hand and arm clearly indicate the direction.

Goal-kick

Corner-kick

Caution or expulsion

With the card system, the card shall be shown in the manner illustrated. The player's identity must be recorded at the same time.

Signals by the Assistant Referees

Off-side
Flag held upright to indicate off-side.

Off-side

When the referee stops play, the assistant referee indicates the position on the far side of the field.

Off-side
Position near the centre of the field.

Off-side

Position on the near side of the field.

Throw-in

Corner-kick

The assistant referee may first need to signal that the ball has gone out of play if there is any doubt. He should also look at the referee in case he has already made his own decision, which may be different from the assistant referee's.

Goal-kick

Substitution

Back view of the assistant referee signalling to the referee for a substitution to be made.

Substitution

Front view of the assistant referee signalling to the refereee when a substitute is waiting at the lines.

Stay Involved with Soccer—Become a Referee

You may know how to play soccer, but do you know the Laws of the Game?

A great way to apply your knowledge and stay involved with the world's most popular sport is to become a soccer referee.

As the number of people playing soccer in the United States continues to grow at a rapid rate, the need for qualified referees and assistant referees also grows at all levels of play—recreational, youth, high school, college, amateur, and even professional.

U.S. Soccer undertook the responsibility in the early 1970s to develop programs for training a large number of referees. The training is conducted by qualified state referee instructors in a consistent manner throughout the nation. Referees are required to attend annual, advanced national training programs. American referees are playing an increasing role in CONCACAF matches and continue to get more and better appointments to work international matches. U.S. Soccer referee membership has been increasing steadily over the past decade and is approximately 88,000. This figure is one of the largest among FIFA member nations.

There are eight different levels for registered referees, ranging from local leagues and organizations to international competitions. Those select referees who attain a ranking from FIFA, the world governing body of soccer, are eligible to referee matches at any one of FIFA's world championships.

If you are interested in learning more about becoming a referee, please fill out the form below and your name will be forwarded to the appropriate referee administrator in your area, or call the U.S. Soccer Referee Department at 312/808-1300.

Name _____

Address _____

City _____

State _____

Zip Code _____

Phone _____

Notes

Notes